"Rockman, McLay, and Freedman have created a wonderful, simple, and practical introduction to mindfulness for our teens who need it now more than ever. Through a range of fun practices, thoughtful reflections, and just the right amount of science, they guide adolescents, and their adults, through a path to create their own sustainable and helpful practice."

—**Christopher Willard, PsyD**, coauthor of *Alphabreaths*

"It's harder than ever to be a teenager—and this gem of a book is full of practical, scientifically based help. It's a great combination of inviting exercises, useful information, and friendly support. A wonderful resource for adolescents and their parents, and for anyone who teaches or works with teens!"

—**Rick Hanson, PhD**, author of *Resilient*

"Teens have had to shoulder a lot during the pandemic, adding more stress to an already challenging developmental period. *The Mindful Teen Workbook* will help them meet life's struggles with greater resilience, and savor its awesome moments more deliberately. Written in an engaging and accessible style, it features carefully calibrated didactic content alongside experiential learning, and guides teens on how show up more fully to their lives and embrace the vast potential that awaits them."

—**Zindel Segal, PhD**, coauthor of *The Mindful Way through Depression*

"Teens are under more pressure today than ever before. This book is a well-written, engaging, and extremely practical resource to help teens cultivate the skills of mindfulness, compassion, emotional resiliency, and metacognitive awareness during a critical time in their development. Mindfulness (as the authors note) is indeed a superpower. As a youth mindfulness researcher, I'm delighted that this workbook offers such an inviting, user-friendly style of teaching mindfulness to teens."

—**Randye J. Semple, PhD**, associate professor at the University of Southern California, and coauthor of *Mindfulness-Based Cognitive Therapy for Anxious Children* and *The Mindfulness Matters Program for Children and Adolescents*

"This book comes out at a time when mindfulness, self-compassion, and well-being are consequential for youth. Kudos to the authors for making mindfulness-based skills accessible for teens. *The Mindful Teen Workbook* advances the mindfulness movement for youth in this book."

—**Gina Biegel, MA, LMFT**, developer of the Mindfulness-Based Stress Reduction for Teens (MBSR-T) program

"Now more than ever, our world needs humans who can tap into their true selves and respond to stress with mindfulness and self-compassion. This workbook supports this need by offering simple practices that help us get to know who we really are at heart so that we can exert our power and freedom to choose exactly how we want to be in relationship to everything around us and within us."

—**Jaisa Sulit, BPHD, BEd, MScOT**, mindful self-compassion and mindfulness-based stress reduction (MBSR) teacher, and author of *Purpose in Paralysis*

"*The Mindful Teen Workbook* is an excellent support for teens. In fact, people of all ages could benefit. The authors translated the wisdom of mindfulness and simplified it into accessible language. Each chapter scaffolds on each other and offers a chance to learn, reflect, practice, and integrate into everyday life. An impressive array of tools that teens can experience individually, with friends, or in a therapeutic context."

—**Shari Geller, PhD**, clinical psychologist, mindful self-compassion teacher, author of *A Practical Guide for Cultivating Therapeutic Presence*, and coauthor of *Therapeutic Presence*

"Mindfulness is a much-needed approach that can help teens navigate through daily challenges, including stress, intense emotions, conflict, overwhelm, and uncertainty. But the key is to make mindfulness demystified, simple, and relevant for each teen. This book accomplishes this in an elegant and thoughtful way, empowering each reader to creatively adapt and make mindfulness their own."

—**Lidia Zylowska, MD**, associate professor at the University of Minnesota Medical School, author of *The Mindfulness Prescription for Adult ADHD*, and coauthor of and *Mindfulness for Adult ADHD*

"A powerful guide for teenagers willing to develop a mindful way of caring for inner experiences, especially when facing challenging moments. Step by step, this workbook helps develop resourceful skills that help teens meet stillness and respond with resilience in the post-pandemic world."

—**Vitor Friary**, author of *Mindfulness for Children*, and founder of the Centro de Mindfulness in Brazil

the mindful teen workbook

powerful skills to find calm,
develop self-compassion
& build resilience

PATRICIA ROCKMAN, MD
ALLISON MᶜLAY, DCS
M. LEE FREEDMAN, MD

Instant Help Books
An Imprint of New Harbinger Publications, Inc.

Copyright © 2022 by Patricia Rockman, Allison McLay, M. Lee Freedman
Instant Help Books
An imprint of New Harbinger Publications, Inc.
5674 Shattuck Avenue
Oakland, CA 94609
www.newharbinger.com

Cover design by Amy Shoup; Acquired by Ryan Buresh; Edited by Karen Schader

Library of Congress Cataloging-in-Publication Data

Names: Rockman, Patricia, author. | McLay, Allison, author. | Freedman, M. Lee, author.
Title: Mindful teen workbook / Patricia Rockman, Allison McLay, M. Lee Freedman.
Description: Oakland, CA : Instant Help Books, an imprint of New Harbinger Publications, Inc., [2022] | Includes bibliographical references.
Identifiers: LCCN 2022018698 | ISBN 9781684039432 (trade paperback)
Subjects: LCSH: Mindfulness (Psychology)--Juvenile literature. | Stress (Psychology)--Juvenile literature. | Self-management (Psychology)--Juvenile literature. | BISAC: YOUNG ADULT NONFICTION / Health & Daily Living / Mindfulness & Meditation | YOUNG ADULT NONFICTION / Inspirational & Personal Growth
Classification: LCC BF637.M56 R63 2022 | DDC 158.1/3--dc23/eng/20220616
LC record available at https://lccn.loc.gov/2022018698

Printed in the United States of America

24   23   22

10   9   8   7   6   5   4   3   2   1   First Printing

For Tita Angangco—Her vision and commitment to making mindfulness accessible to all people created the foundation for us to write this book.

Patricia Rockman

Allison McLay

M. Lee Freedman

contents

introduction: why this mindful workbook for teens?

Mindfulness has gone mainstream, but what is all the buzz about, and why develop a workbook especially for teens? For young people, there are particular challenges and opportunities in discovering what mindfulness has to offer. Sitting still and meditating may not be the most accessible or engaging way for some young people to develop the skills and attitudes of mindfulness. Luckily, there are other ways to learn the mindful skills and attitudes that can be helpful in negotiating the turmoil, stress, and excitement of this time of life.

How does this work? Mindfulness helps you understand your own experience—both the pleasant and the difficult. It's a process of exploration that involves learning to work with your attention in a particular way so you can direct it when and how you want. The practices and exercises in this book give you tools for understanding and managing thoughts, emotions, and behaviors so they don't control you. Writing down your responses to the exercises will help you clarify your thinking, gain perspective, remember what you have learned, and help you see that you are not your thoughts. The awareness or understanding you get in the process allows for more choice in how you can respond.

Developing these mindful tools can make it easier to take in the awesome when it happens, handle stressful situations with more resilience, and strengthen your relationships. Since you're in a period of major growth and development, it's a great time to make positive changes in the way you interact with yourself and others.

The ideas for this workbook grew out of programs for youth we developed through the Centre for Mindfulness Studies in Toronto, where we realized that a fresh approach was necessary. We hope to engage you with mindful ideas, attitudes, and exercises in a spirit of discovery and exploration. The workbook presents reflective activities and practices that focus on awareness and the senses, the brain as friend or foe, difficult mind and mood states, choosing your response versus reacting, building resilience, and relating mindfully to others and the world. We hope that this will be a helpful journey and that you will be inspired to keep learning and creating a mindful life.

PS. If you're an adult—a helping professional who's interested in using this workbook with the teens in your life—you can download a free guide to using this workbook in groups at http://www.newharbinger.com/49432.

CHAPTER 1

A Mindful Beginning

Mindfulness is a skill, a way of being that helps you get to know your inner world. With mindful awareness, you can live more joyfully and cope with life's difficulties in more adaptive ways than using the unhelpful strategies we often use to deal with problems, especially when we get overwhelmed. Mindfulness is about becoming aware of your moment-to-moment experience without giving yourself a hard time. You learn to put your attention where you want it, rather than it mindlessly going all over the place. Mindfulness is an active process that promotes resilience and supports wellness. While it takes practice, it can be learned and gives you more options about how to live a kinder, more engaged life.

1 meeting your inner world

what to know

Mindfulness is a superpower. It helps us attend to the ordinary in extraordinary ways. Being able to direct our attention to where we choose through mindfulness increases our options about what we want to do, if anything. This skill can help us meet life stressors with more resilience. Before we dive in, it will help to understand what mindfulness is and what it isn't. So, what is mindfulness?

- Mindfulness involves training your attention so you can be attuned to your outer world through your senses. This attunement allows you to really connect with yourself, others, and the world around you.

- It's a skill that can help us identify and describe our thoughts, emotions, body sensations, and actions or urges (even those we don't like) so that we can get to know our inner world. After all, knowledge is power.

- It's also a tool to help us see how our minds have a life of their own, how they get caught in worry, planning, the past, repetitive thinking, and so much more.

- It helps us meet difficult mental, emotional, and physical states and get to know when we are beyond our ability to manage them. It can help to keep us from getting overwhelmed.

Okay, now you know a bit about what mindfulness is, so let's look at what it's not.

- Mindfulness is not about relaxation (although it can be about creating more ease) or about simply finding your bliss.

- It's not about avoiding the things we don't like by distracting ourselves.

- It's not about sitting on a cushion or breathing with your eyes closed, although this can be part of it. It's also not a religion.

Mindfulness, then, is about waking up to living rather than sleepwalking your way through life. It helps us pay attention to what is actually happening in the moment instead of getting caught up in the stories we tell ourselves, reacting, and getting overwhelmed. Who wouldn't want to be more open, to see things more clearly and perhaps have more joy? This is what can come with a mindfulness practice.

Mindfulness helped Amanda open herself to fears she had:

> When I was younger some kids once put a worm down my back. After that I was always scared of yucky bugs, worms, frogs, mice, and other tiny crawling, flying, or hopping creatures. Once, during a mindfulness seeing practice, I saw a small brown tree frog. It was sitting in the grass, minding its own business. Even though I was nervous, I decided to pay attention and get really curious about it, to get to know it by exploring its shape, color, size, movement. It just sat there quietly. Feeling calm, I picked it up. Amazingly, the frog showed no fear. It just sat in my hand while I held it and looked at it for a long time. I could see that it wasn't scary at all. It was just a frog. Finally, I gently put it down, letting it go. Mindfulness helped me get beyond the stories I had been telling myself and see such creatures in a new way.

Now that you have a better sense of what mindfulness is and isn't, let's try this first mindfulness practice to see how it works.

what to try

Take five minutes to get to know what's going on inside and outside you; you can set a timer if you like. Take a seat or lie down. Get comfortable and close your eyes fully or keep them half-open in a soft, unfocused gaze (you can do this for many practices in the book). Check in to see what you notice about your body. What sensations are showing up? Can you name them—pressure, tension, relaxation, for instance? What sounds can you hear, if any? Are they loud, soft, near, far, high- or low-pitched? If your eyes are open, what do you see? Are you noticing colors, shapes, patterns? Are you noticing any smells around you? Are they pleasant or unpleasant, or are there no particular smells at all? Any thoughts coming up as images? As sentences? Any emotions? These are usually described in single words—glad, sad, mad, scared, bored, disgusted… What do you want to do—urges/impulses—if anything? See if you can identify what's happening in these parts of your inner and outer world, and then write it down when the five minutes is up.

Body sensations: _____

Sounds, sights, smells: _____

Thoughts: _____

Emotions: _____

Urges/impulses: _____

What did you learn while writing this down, if anything?

_____

_____

_____

_____

_____

Let's try another!

more to try

Paying attention in this mindful way to what is going on in your inner world is a useful skill. It provides information that can help you figure out what you need to or might want to do in any given situation. Let's try a couple of examples where you can practice this skill.

Closing your eyes, think of a time when you felt really mad. Try to see all the details of the experience. There's no need to write down the actual situation. Just bring it to mind and focus on what you were thinking. What emotions showed up? What sensations showed up in your body, and what did you do?

_____

_____

_____

_____

_____

On a scale of 1 (very difficult) to 10 (extremely easy), rate how easy it was for you to identify your thoughts, emotions, and body sensations.

Thoughts

Very difficult   Extremely easy

1 ————————————————————————————————— 10

Emotions

Very difficult   Extremely easy

1 ————————————————————————————————— 10

Body Sensations

Very difficult   Extremely easy

1 ————————————————————————————————— 10

Closing your eyes again, think of a time when you had to do or learn something and you felt calm or in a pretty good state. What were you thinking? What emotions showed up? How did your body feel and what did you do? Now, write all this down.

_____

_____

_____

_____

_____

_____

On a scale of 1(very difficult) to 10 (extremely easy), rate how easy it was for you to identify your thoughts, emotions, and body sensations.

Thoughts

Very difficult   Extremely easy

1 ── 10

Emotions

Very difficult   Extremely easy

1 ── 10

Body Sensations

Very difficult   Extremely easy

1 ── 10

See if there is a difference between what you noticed when you were calm and when you were distressed. Were specific aspects of the experiences (thoughts, emotions, body sensations) easier or more difficult to identify? Sometimes it's not so easy to know what's going on in our inner world. It gets easier with practice.

Why might it be useful to develop this skill? Write down some thoughts here.

_____

_____

_____

_____

_____

_____

more to try

In this activity, you will be learning to deliberately direct your attention to a particular body sensation—the sensations of breathing. When your mind wanders or your attention gets pulled away, this common mindfulness practice allows you to notice where the attention automatically goes. In real time, you get to understand how your mind works. You get to know the "habits" of your mind and to become aware of body sensations, thoughts, and emotions that are coming and going. This information is all useful for knowing your inner world. As you notice the movement of attention and consistently bring it back to the sensations of breathing, you are also learning to be in charge of your attention.

Try this short mindfulness breath practice and see what you notice. You will likely find that it's not so easy to pay attention on purpose, but stick with it even if you have to redirect your attention back to the breath many times. You may notice frustration, distraction, restlessness, and lots more. Noticing when your attention moves is as important as returning it to the sensations of breathing. It's all part of what you can learn about your inner world, while also training your brain to pay attention.

Some people may feel overwhelmed or uncomfortable with breath practices. If this happens to you, you can stop the practice, or use another anchor for your attention like sensations in the hands or feet.

You can follow these basic written instructions or, even better, you can listen to the recording provided online at http://www.newharbinger.com/49432. Once you get familiar with the instructions, you can simply guide yourself through the practice, perhaps using a timer on your phone to know when five or ten minutes of practice is up.

- Get comfortable either lying down or sitting with your back upright, feet on the floor in a posture that is alert but relaxed. Close your eyes fully if that's comfortable for you, or keep them half-open in a soft, unfocused gaze. Become aware of your entire body from head to toe.

- Now direct your attention to the sensations of breathing. Not thinking about breathing, but feeling the sensations in the body as you breathe in and breathe out. Find the place where you feel those sensations most clearly. It could be at the nostrils, the chest and rib cage, or the belly. Choose this place and focus your attention there.

- Get curious about those sensations. Can you stay with them for a full in-breath and a full out-breath, or more? Can you get really precise in noticing sensations? You may become aware of the flow of air at the nostrils, or the body expanding or rising on an inhale at the chest or belly and falling back when you breathe out.

- You may find that the attention moves or gets pulled away from the sensations of breathing quite automatically—into sounds; thinking; other body sensations; perhaps with emotions, reactions, self-talk; maybe self-judgment. This movement is normal and very useful to notice. Simply recognize where the attention has gone and gently, without any judgment or other self-talk about it, return the attention to the sensations of breath at your chosen place in the body.

- See if you can simply practice paying attention to the sensations of breath for a few minutes, directing the attention back there as often as needed when it moves to something else.

- When you are ready, or the timer goes off, expand your attention to a sense of your entire body once again, and reorient yourself to your surroundings.

It can be hard to guide yourself. One way to do that is to hold a structure of the practice in mind: posture (1 minute), breathe, return to breath (over and over for 4 minutes), sense the entire body (1 minute), end.

On the following lines, jot down anything you noticed during this awareness of breath practice.

_____

_____

_____

_____

_____

_____

It's useful to know what's going on in your internal world because this information helps you make better plans and decisions. Seeing your inner world clearly is mindful awareness, and the best way to find out how it works is to practice. As we begin, it can be good to plan what changes you would like to work toward with the awareness you are developing, and we will do that next.

2 creating your intentions

what to know

Your intentions set a direction and involve a commitment to engage in the practices and exercises in this workbook, and in your daily life. What would be your reasons for engaging in this learning? What would you want to be different or better? For example, you may want to have better relationships, feel less stressed, or worry less. Thinking about your intentions and writing them down can act as a guide to help you stay on track.

Making your intentions concrete (describable), small, and stated in positive terms can keep them manageable and make it more likely you will follow through. For example, if you want to feel less stressed, you might think about what would be different if you were calmer. This approach goes for mindfulness practice and for anything else we are trying to do or learn.

what to try

Write down what you hope to get from learning mindfulness. You can check back to Practice 1 to review its benefits, which include being able to manage difficult emotions, becoming less reactive, and getting more joy out of life, to name a few.

_____

_____

_____

Mindfulness is both a skill and a practice. When we learn anything new, we are often faced with challenges. These challenges are part of the learning process. Being able to identify them and learning to work with them can help keep you from getting discouraged. Write down any concerns or challenges you might have in doing the practices in this workbook and how you might respond to them.

_____

_____

_____

Name some strengths and supports that you bring to help you with your aims.

_____

_____

_____

more to try

If you have difficulty deciding on what you want from practicing mindfulness, try closing your eyes, taking a few deep breaths, and imagining what may be different when you are finished with the workbook.

How will you know that you are on the right track?

_____

_____

_____

What kinds of thoughts and emotions would you hope to have?

_____

_____

_____

Take a few minutes to imagine yourself going through your day. What do you see happening?

_____

_____

_____

_____

If you like to express your ideas visually, you can take a few minutes and draw what it will look like when you're using mindfulness in your daily life.

CHAPTER 2

What's Going On Now?

Much of the time, we are automatically reacting to whatever is coming our way, without being aware of what is going on inside and outside us. Mindfulness is all about developing more awareness and getting good information, which allows us to make skillful choices about how we interact with the world and others. We get this information by paying attention to what is actually happening for us at the moment. What state are we in? Are we calm, stressed, busy with planning, worried, upset? What attitude is guiding our thinking and actions in any given moment? What is going on around us? We can access all kinds of information from our senses. In this chapter, we will look at how to tune into what is happening so that we can respond on purpose, not on automatic pilot.

3 being and doing

what to know

There are two main ways we interact with the world: "doing mode" and "being mode," and this distinction is supported by what we know about the brain. Doing mode is about getting things done. We need it for things like planning, organizing, remembering, and analyzing, and we use it deliberately or automatically to accomplish tasks and attain goals. We also need it for problem solving. However, problem solving in this mode can result in a lot of challenging and unnecessary mental activity, such as worry, overthinking, or going over and over some past event—all with no benefit, particularly when we are dealing with difficult emotions. In doing mode, we often get stuck in anxious thinking, regretting, judging, personalizing, or jumping to conclusions.

We also have a being mode—a state where we are tuned into what is in our experience in real time, being more receptive, or taking in, rather than getting caught up in what it means for us or what needs to be done. A way to access being mode is by paying attention to the senses or sensations, with a focus on what's there and without jumping to judgment or analysis. Switching into being mode can disrupt some of the habitual negative mental activity of doing mode.

These modes involve different parts and functions of the brain, and we need both of them. With mindful awareness, we can learn to intentionally choose our mode based on what is going to be helpful for the task at hand or for what we need. This table breaks down the main aspects of each mode.

Doing mode	Being mode
Focusing on what needs to be done	Focusing on receiving information (as sensations)
Going through the motions on our usual autopilot: working, eating, walking, talking, and so on based on our default "wiring"	Attending on purpose to the present as it is unfolding
Works through thinking Helpful—problem solving, analyzing, drawing conclusions, interpretations Unhelpful—worry, repetitive thinking, interpretations (Interpretations can be helpful or unhelpful)	Paying attention to the senses and body sensations—smell, touch, sight, sound, taste, present moment observation (always in the *now*)
Focusing on past and future	Focusing on seeing what is here *now* in our direct experience Perceiving the moment, whether wanted, neutral, or unwanted
Dissatisfaction with what is (wanting/ not wanting; should not/should be) Often a treadmill of judgment (of self, others, the world)	Open to what is here; curious Deferring judgment about whether experience is good or bad

Now that you have a rough idea of what the being and doing modes are, you may be wondering what they look like in real life, or how they might impact the quality of your experience. Consider Taylor's experience of the doing mode while looking in the mirror:

Oh, my face is terrible—look how fat it is. I look like a fat baby. So unattractive! I don't deserve to be loved. No one will ever want to have sex with me. If I could only lose ten pounds, I'd be okay. I'd be attractive. But it won't be enough. Even when I was skeletal, I wanted to lose more. It's so messed up.

Note the negative, harsh judgment of the self. Notice the problem solving and the worry. This is doing mode at its worst.

Through mindfulness practice, Taylor found ways to short-circuit doing mode:

It's so hard for me to get out of this state once I'm in it. When I can pick up my guitar and play "Little Wing," I hear the notes and the words in my head. I feel my fingers moving over the strings. I'm here just playing.

In being mode, while playing guitar, Taylor's repetitive, negative thinking or storytelling is disrupted, and they have literally come to their senses.

Let's now explore these two modes with an exercise.

what to try

Choosing a mode is not as simple as separating doing from being. Wouldn't that be nice! However, you can change your experience by noticing what you're paying attention to and whether you're doing so on purpose or it's just happening automatically. By paying attention, you can see whether you're in doing or being mode and learn to know when one mode might be more useful than the other.

For example, let's say it's time to get dressed for the day. Circle the mode or modes you might choose if you were aware of what was going on.

Helpful doing (planning, organizing, decision making): You see what you like, what might look good, and what might be okay for the weather outside.

Unhelpful doing (worrying, judging): You're stressing about how you will look. Is your outfit cool enough? You start thinking about needing different clothes or about your body image.

Being: You notice your thinking and start paying attention to the color or feel of the clothing and to the weather outside, and you focus on the process of getting *dressed*.

So, in the first example (helpful doing), you can use your thinking brain to make decisions that help you get dressed and get out of the house. In the second (unhelpful doing), you're on the way to getting stuck in a loop of negative thinking that may make you sad or anxious. Those thoughts don't actually help you get out the door.

If you catch this happening, what can you do? Is it time to give your doing mind a break? Try switching into being mode (the third example). Paying attention to the senses and to the feel and look of what is actually around you in that moment, and disrupting some automatic, emotionally loaded thoughts, is a choice you can make with practice.

When would it be helpful to be in doing mode? (For example, studying, fixing your bike, planning a party)

_____

_____

_____

When would it be helpful to be in being mode? (For example, listening to music, eating a snack, appreciating a beautiful day)

_____

_____

_____

When might doing mode be a problem? (For example, when you are stressed about a deadline or worried about a relationship)

_____

_____

_____

What part of doing mode could get in the way? Think about judgments about yourself or others, the anxious and automatic thoughts, or repetitive thinking that can make it hard to think clearly or make good choices. It may feel productive—but is it?

_____

_____

_____

When might being mode be a problem? (For example, when you are listening to music, into the pleasure of it, and not finishing that homework or task for the next day)

_____

_____

_____

more to try

STOP is a well-known mindfulness practice that can help you see what mode you are in and get curious about it. It can help you determine if the mode you're in is what you really want and need at that moment.

S top whatever you are doing.

T ake a few breaths.
Notice sensations of breathing to settle your attention.

O bserve your thoughts, emotions, and body sensations.

P roceed with more awareness into your next moments.

These examples show how Blake used the STOP practice:

I'm having a good time right now shooting hoops. I'm going to use STOP and take it in. He takes a couple of deep breaths to slow things down and pays attention for a moment to his inner world. *I'm having good thoughts about being here now and the people I'm with...I like them and they like being with me. I feel content and sort of happy. My body feels relaxed and loose. This is nice to notice...*

My mom is yelling at me to get off my phone cause it's dinner. I'm getting pissed off. I'm going to STOP and check this out, inside me. I'll take a couple of deeper breaths. I'm thinking "Leave me alone. What's the big deal...I'm doing something." I'm irritated and angry. I feel tight in my body and my face is scrunched up. I think, "So what do you want to do now?"

Using STOP didn't fix this situation, but it gave Blake a pause to reset a bit and not just react without thinking. He was in a better position to choose how he was going to respond.

4 working with the senses

what to know

Our body sensations and our five senses—what we see, hear, smell, taste, and touch—are always happening in the now and are available to us. After all, you take your body with you wherever you go. Really paying attention to the senses and our sensations, and their qualities, is a key mindfulness tool that allows us to switch out of doing mode into being mode. Attending to sensations helps keep us from getting lost in our thoughts about the past and future, where thinking often goes to regret or worry. We have another place—the body and senses—to put our attention rather than getting caught up in our minds. It can also allow us to tap into the pleasures of being present. Let's try giving your doing mind a break today!

what to try

Here are a few ways to get into being mode by playing with your senses. Closing your eyes for all or some of each exercise can intensify what you notice.

Seeing: Close your eyes for a few moments. Now open them and look around you. What are you seeing right now? Drop the thoughts about what you are seeing and just notice what you actually see, whatever is there—colors (red, blue, orange), shapes (squares, rectangles, circles), sheen, shadow, movement... Write down some of what you see.

_____

_____

_____

_____

Hearing: Paying attention to sounds can be an easy way to move into being mode. Turn on some music and bring all your attention to just hearing. What's the tone, pitch, volume, tempo, and the sound of individual instruments?

_____

_____

_____

_____

Smelling and Tasting: When you peel an orange, you can notice the citrus smell, and when you taste it, the burst of juicy flavor. Choose a food you would like to practice with. Before you take the first bite, really smell it, and focus on the sensations. What do you smell? Can you describe these sensations? What do you taste? Can you describe the flavors?

_____

_____

_____

_____

Touching: The human sense of touch is very well developed, like a dog's sense of smell. Take an object you like the feel of, such as a soft blanket, a smooth rock, or a piece of clothing. Focus on the sense of touch. Can you describe the sensations, such as softness or smoothness?

_____

_____

_____

_____

more to try

Learning to pay attention to your sensations when doing an activity can help you focus. Paying attention in this way can be a place to come back to when your attention has a mind of its own. Attention can go many places, some nice and others not so much.

Do you often find yourself bored or miserable while doing some task, like washing dishes? Where is your attention? What is occupying your mind? Instead, imagine if you instead paid attention to the feeling of warm, soapy water on your skin, to the sound of the tap running, to the feeling of your hands going through the motions of washing or scrubbing. You may also, at times, be enjoying a moment, such as lying in the sun. You could get even more pleasure by tuning into the feel of the sun on your skin or how relaxed your body feels. There may be many opportunities to have a different experience just by paying attention to what you're doing in a different way—using the senses.

Pick an everyday activity (like doing a chore, eating, walking, dancing) and spend a few moments tuning into your senses. Get curious and see what you notice. What are the qualities of those sensations? They may not all be pleasant. See if you can pick one that you find positive and one you find negative. Jot down any observations you remember from trying this activity. They can come from sight, touch, hearing, smell, or taste, or from sensations coming from inside the body.

Activity	What you noticed	Was it positive (+) or negative (-)?
Walking this morning	Cool—breeze on face	+
	Loudness—noise from traffic	−

You can pay attention to your senses any time you remember, and you'll be practicing mindfulness when you do so.

being the boss of your brain 5

what to know

For some very good reasons, our brains pay special attention to negative experiences. As humans evolved, it was helpful to focus on threats or danger. For example, if you wanted to survive, it was important to know the signs that a predator was nearby.

Positive experiences aren't registered with the same intensity. Positive experiences were unlikely to affect whether you lived to see another day. As a result, our ancestors—and people to this day—focus much more on the negative. This negativity bias is hardwired in our brain to the point where we often see things as negative when they're not. Our brains also can't tell the difference between a real threat, like stepping into the road in busy traffic, or a false alarm. A false alarm could be reacting as if something is dangerous or threatening even if it isn't, or worrying about something bad that might happen. Both feel very real to us. Because of this, our minds are often preoccupied with negative thoughts and fears. These ideas usually don't actually help us survive, but they do make life more miserable.

What does negativity bias look like in action? Here's how Brittney experienced it:

> *I walk out of my apartment and, at the elevator, I see something big and black on the floor. There's no thinking. It's just like a startle reflex; a jolt. Even a little jump. That's like a second. Maybe less. Then the next second is "AH! WHAT IS IT? IS IT A SPIDER?! A THREAT?!" And heart racing, breathing fast, lots of tension… Then suddenly, "It's a GLOVE" and I think, "Oh—ha-ha, I'm so dumb—anxiety is so silly—lol," and I can laugh at it. And the physical reactions fade but that takes a minute or so.*

And it takes four times of passing that glove in the hallway before Brittney has no startle reaction at all. It fades in steps:

First time: As above

Second time: Oh ha–ha, it's the stupid glove. (Her fear response is a little less intense.)

Third time: Goddamn glove! (Her fear response is even smaller.)

Fourth time: Glove, grumble, grumble (Still smaller.)

With mindfulness, we can catch these negative automatic reactions, this tendency to jump into harsh thoughts or emotions directed at the situation or ourselves. We can deliberately check in and ask, "Who is the boss of my brain right now?" Doing mode is often busy with false alarms, while being mode is more in the flow of experience as it shows up in the moment, registering what is actually there. Are we stuck in a negative loop, or are we open to what is happening in the here and now? Can we bring a more open, receptive, neutral stance to what we experience?

To get less stuck in the negativity bias we have to "rewire" our brains to balance paying attention to the positive or neutral with the need to stay safe by taking in potential or actual danger. This rewiring can help improve our mood, increase our resilience, and boost our enjoyment in living. Thanks to *neuroplasticity* (the brain's ability to keep changing based on experience or repetition), we can change our brains with practice, and choose the mode we want or need to be in (Hanson 2009). First, we have to be aware of what's happening to become the boss of our own brains. Let's try an exercise that will give us more practice in paying attention to positive experiences.

what to try

To balance out our negativity bias, it helps to give your full attention to positive experiences—even for a few moments. You have to catch yourself having a good time. You need to focus on what thoughts are around, name the positive emotions that are present (joy, satisfaction, pleasure), check in with sensations showing up in the body and describe them (light, relaxed, tingling), and really soak in the experience. By staying with the experience and sensing it in your body, you will be creating new pathways in your brain for taking in the good or even the awesome, but this takes time and repetition.

For practice, think about something positive that happened today or in the recent past, no matter how small as long as it's something you enjoyed. Bring the situation to mind and write down your thoughts, your emotions, and your physical sensations, and add any reflections you have.

practice 5 ✳ being the boss of your brain

Situation:_____

_____

Thoughts: _____

_____

Emotions: _____

_____

Physical sensations: _____

_____

Reflections: _____

_____

more to try

Think of a person, a pet, or a celebrity that makes you happy:_____

Name something you appreciate about the room you are currently in:

_____

Name something you love to eat: _____

Think of a recent time you felt really good, really happy, and write down everything (in sentences or words) you can remember about that time (where you were, what you noticed, saw, heard, felt). No event is too small.

_____

_____

_____

Any thoughts about how it felt doing this exercise? Any ideas about what you noticed?

_____

_____

_____

_____

Now look for future opportunities to take in the good or awesome and rewire your brain for positivity.

6 give me attitude

what to know

Learning to pay attention is important, but equally important is how we pay attention. Our attitudes shape our experience, often in a positive or negative way. They can be a conscious choice. More often they are a habit—the way we have learned to respond, whether it's helpful or not.

With mindfulness, it's all about awareness, and the possibility of seeing or responding to things in a fresh way when we want or need to. We step back and recognize what attitude we are bringing to a situation, such as a challenge, a relationship, how we talk to ourselves. If we see that an attitude is getting in our way, we can experiment with practicing a different attitude, and see what comes of it. For example, practicing an attitude of patience with oneself or others may open up some opportunities that could be shut down quickly if we reacted with frustration, negative judgments, and anxiety. Attitudes such as curiosity, kindness, nonjudgment, and patience are fundamental; they are our allies (friends) in developing mindfulness (Kabat-Zinn 1990; Woods, Rockman, and Collins 2019).

what to try

Some attitudes support our goal of being mindful, especially when we're struggling with tough emotions or states. Other attitudes limit our view and experience, shutting us down to possibilities. Here are definitions of several important mindful attitudes that can be helpful:

nonjudging—not immediately judging people, things, or situations as good or bad or as what we like or don't like

patience—being okay with things taking time

beginner's mind—approaching experiences without thinking you already know what's going on

trust—confidence in the dependability of yourself and others

nonstriving—being okay with not trying to get anywhere

acceptance—willingness to see and be with things as they are, as a first reaction

letting go—not holding on to unhelpful thoughts, emotions, relationships, behaviors, or situations

curiosity—taking an interest in and exploring experience, situations, and the natural world

compassion—empathy for and the desire to help yourself and/or others

Match each attitude with the definition that best describes it by drawing a line between them:

Curiosity	Seeing things anew
Nonjudging	Not pushing to get somewhere
Patience	Letting things be as they are
Trust	To stop hanging on or resisting
Compassion	Staying calm while waiting
Nonstriving	Not evaluating as good or bad
Letting go	Caring for a person's suffering and wishing to help
Acceptance	Placing confidence in
Beginner's mind	Taking an interest

Now that you know what mindful attitudes are, let's practice working with them.

more to try

Pick an activity that is new for you or often seems hard, and results in a certain amount of struggle and negative reactions. For example, you might choose to solve a difficult puzzle (crossword, Sudoku); play an instrument you don't know well; or try to write, draw, or color with your nondominant hand.

Do the activity for five to ten minutes and observe what comes up in terms of your attitude, which may be reflected by thoughts or emotions. Name the emotions if you can (for example, "Frustration is here." or "Pride is here."). See what thoughts come up (for example, "I'm no good at this." "This is interesting." "This is too hard." "This isn't so hard."). Can you name the attitudes you experienced, knowing these may be the opposite of mindful attitudes?

Now stay with the same activity for another five to ten minutes, seeing if you can practice patience with yourself and the task and get curious about the process (for example, "Why is it difficult?" "What do I expect to happen?" "What is the result of the way I'm reacting?" "How is this different from other things I do?"). Write down what you observe related to your attitudes and how they shift, if they do, when you bring curiosity and patience to a situation.

_____

_____

_____

_____

_____

_____

After doing these practices, can you imagine how bringing mindful attitudes to experience might be helpful?

At this point we have introduced you to some mindful ideas and tools, such as how to investigate your inner and outer experience, the difference between doing mode and being mode, paying attention to your senses to be in the present moment, working with mindful attitudes, and using the awareness of breath practice. Now it's time to move from your inner world to what shakes your world and see how to use what you have learned so far.

CHAPTER 3

About Stress

Being human doesn't come with an owner's manual. We have to figure out how to troubleshoot. Experiencing stress is part of being human—an inescapable and necessary part of living and growing. But it can also be harmful and wear us down. With some knowledge and self-awareness, we can learn how to deal with stress as well as possible. Using mindful skills and attitudes helps us recognize when we are heading into difficulty with stress and gives us clues about what we need to do.

7 am I stressed?

what to know

Before learning some strategies for dealing with stress, you need to know how it shows up for you. How do you know you are stressed? You can get clues about what state you're in, and whether you're stressed or not, by noticing what thoughts, emotions, body sensations, and urges are present. You have been working with this in the first two chapters, and you can also fine-tune this skill by getting more specific about what is happening in your state. We can apply this awareness skill as a strategy for dealing with stress. However, a first step is to practice checking in when we are stressed and not stressed (not emotionally charged or activated), so we know the difference.

what to try

Our states, like the weather, are always changing. On any day you could go from feeling calm to stressed to excited to bored, and so on. The emotions, thoughts, body sensations, and urges that go with these states come and go, like clouds.

Based on your experience right now, identify what's happening inside you as precisely as possible. Draw four clouds to represent thoughts, emotions, body sensations, and urges. Then write in what you notice is going on in these areas right this minute. You may not have things to write in every cloud. You can use the table of emotions and body sensations as a reference to get more specific, and feel free to add your own. After doing this activity, you may get a sense of whether you are in a stressed state.

The following table links primary (basic) and secondary (more complex) emotions with some associated body sensations. This linkage is good to be aware of because the body can let us know what we are feeling. Note that we often have body sensations without emotions and may also have emotions without body sensations. There are many other sensations and emotions not listed here that you may identify over time. We are building a vocabulary of experience. This table is a guide to help with that process.

Emotions and Body Sensations

Primary emotion	Secondary emotions	Body sensations
Fear	Scared, anxious, insecure, threatened, nervous, overwhelmed, vulnerable	Shaky, sweaty, numb, trembling, breathless, tense, tight chest, agitated, restless, racing heart, pit in the stomach
Sadness	Lonely, hurt, depressed, grief, shame, embarrassed, remorseful, disappointed	Heavy, tearful, tight throat or chest, low energy, congested, shoulders dropping, head dropping, face flushing, mouth drooping
Anger	Mad, frustrated, critical, aggressive, let down, jealous, disrespected, resentful, annoyed, irritated, betrayed	Hot, energized, forehead tight, jaw clenched, tension in the diaphragm, impulse to hit, increased heart rate
Joy	Happy, content, playful, interested, accepted, creative, joyful, confident, loving	Body lightness, relaxed muscles, energized, warm-hearted
Disgust	Repelled, disapproving, appalled, revolted, hesitant, judgmental, bored	Constricting, gagging sensation, nauseous, body leaning away
Surprise	Startled, excited, confused, amazed, shocked	Full of energy, alert, wide-eyed, short breaths
Trust	Accepting, admiring, calm, peaceful	Relaxed, body at ease, shoulders soft, slower breathing
Anticipation	Interested, curious, vigilant	Alert, energized, quicker breathing, body tingling

8 getting to know stress

what to know

How many times have you said or heard someone say, "I'm soooooo stressed out"? But what does the word "stress" even mean? We can think of it as the body's reaction to a perceived demand that we have to adapt or respond to in some way (Selye 1973). We refer to this demand as a *stressor*, which is something that causes a stress reaction and can be external or internal. An external stressor comes from something outside us (starting a new relationship, money, work or school issues, time pressure, and so on). An internal stressor comes from inside us (thoughts, emotions, body sensations).

Stress reactions show up automatically in many systems of the body. They can increase our heart rate, speed up our breathing, make our muscles tense, and turn off our digestion (giving us an upset stomach). Stress reactions can get us physically ready to fight or to run away (you may have heard this referred to as "fight or flight"), and at other times the reaction might be to freeze or shut down, even if what we are stressed by requires none of these things. These reactions help keep us humans alive when we are confronted by danger, but too much of this stress reaction, caused by too many things, can be harmful.

We can also have "good" stress reactions, like when we are excited or revved up about something we want to do, a new relationship, or learning to play a game or sport. There is an optimal level of stress that can be motivating and help us function. Too much stress for too long can be overwhelming, and can decrease motivation and functioning.

Stress reactions often show up as a tangled mess. As a first step in getting to know our stress reactions and how we can manage them, separating them out into their components (thoughts, emotions, body sensations, and behaviors) can be a useful skill to help us decide whether a stress reaction is a friend or foe.

what to try

Getting to know our stress signs means bringing attention to body sensations, thoughts, emotions, and behaviors when stress shows up, in order to tease apart the web of reactivity. Try filling in the following web, identifying what you think happens to people when they are in a stressed state.

Web of Reactivity

STRESS

Thoughts

Emotions

Body
Sensations

Behaviors

We need to learn when stress is a friend and when it's causing us problems. To do this, we need to get to know our personal stress signs, both positive and negative, which we'll explore in this exercise.

Recall a time when you were in a stressed state about something positive and it was making you feel nervous. For example, maybe you were performing at a concert or competing in a sport. Write down how this stress showed up in your body, thoughts, emotions, and actions.

_____

_____

Next, remember a recent time when you felt mad or were worried about something. Try to bring up an example that is not too intense, like a 3 or 4 out of 10, and not likely to feel overwhelming. (If you find that you are exploring an issue that is too emotionally charged, feel free to stop and take a few deep breaths, pick something lighter, or try another time.) Write down your own stress signals. What body sensations were present? What emotions? What thoughts? What urges did you have or actions did you take?

_____

_____

Now look at what you wrote down to describe positive stress and negative stress. What differences and similarities can you see? Try to identify what made it a friend or foe. Getting to know our different stress reactions or signals can increase our awareness, helping us be mindful about what is going on, and what we need to do about it, if anything.

_____

_____

more to try

Stress is often associated with emotions, which can provide a strong signal. Try this exercise to get to know your emotions and how they come and go, and how outside factors can bring them up. Identifying emotions and how they work can help us catch them before they take over.

Choose three songs that reflect the emotions listed below. Get settled for a couple of minutes, closing your eyes and checking in with how your body feels right now. Open your eyes and turn on the sad song. Then close your eyes again, and while you listen to the song, pay attention to your physical sensations and emotions. When the song is finished, write down what you noticed. Do this with each song. (You can refer to the table of emotions and body sensations from Practice 7.)

Sad song: _____

_____

Angry or agitated song: _____

_____

Happy song: _____

_____

Developing this skill of clearly identifying your emotions is an act of mindfulness and builds awareness skills. You have to know your emotional state before you can do anything about it. This is one way to help you be the boss of your own brain.

9 mindful check-in

what to know

We've been developing the ability to pay attention to and identify our emotions, thoughts, and body sensations. When we try this in the moment, or in real time, we can see that we are usually reacting to something—the good, the bad, and the ugly (like the characters in the movie). Your busy brain is often on automatic, acting all by itself. It has a built-in tendency to focus on what it perceives as wrong, disturbing, or threatening, whether it's real or a false alarm. We can learn to shift out of this habit to take in the good, and sometimes even the awesome, when it is there. We can also notice difficult states and make deliberate choices about what we pay attention to and need. In other words, you can be the boss of your brain instead of it bossing you. Let's try another short mindfulness practice that can help you check in with where you are at and figure out what would be a helpful next step.

what to try

The mindful check-in can help you move out of automatic and into paying attention on purpose (inspired by Segal et al. 2002, 2013). You can then learn to move your attention to where you want it, instead of where your attention wants you. This means learning to both zoom in close to what's going on and then zoom out to get the bigger picture. You can use this skill whenever you think of it, anywhere, anytime—out for a walk, before you go to sleep, waiting in line, or riding the bus. It's a skill, like any other, that you get better at with practice, and it's as simple as 1-2-3. Each step might take about a minute.

You can learn the steps by using the text below or listening to the recording you can download at http://www.newharbinger.com/49432. Once you've learned to guide yourself though this practice, you can use it whenever you want to check in.

Pause and observe what you are experiencing in the moment (naming thoughts, emotions, body sensations).

Shift your focus to the sensations of breathing at the belly, as an anchor for attention (away from whatever was occupying it before).

Widen your attention to be more open, including your whole body, a new start where you might take in more of what is happening in and around you.

Short mindfulness practices like the mindful check-in and STOP develop the skills and awareness you need to actually manage stress reactions when they happen. Building this awareness helps you see the effects of stress early and clearly, so you catch it before it becomes a bigger problem and can choose the most helpful response. In the next chapter, you'll identify your personal stressors and your current coping tools. You'll also learn additional mindfulness tools you can use to manage stress more successfully.

CHAPTER 4

Dealing with Stress

You have been developing some new tools for paying attention and recognizing that you're in a stressed state—knowing how stress shows up in your body, thoughts, and emotions. This recognition gives you more options about when and how you are going to respond and what you need to do to take care of yourself. Some more knowledge, mindful awareness, and strategies are offered in this chapter for dealing with stress.

10 when stress goes bad

what to know

To have good skills for dealing with stress, you have been learning to recognize what it looks like for you in your body and mind. Another thing you need to know is how you are currently dealing with it. Even though you may wish you could get rid of it, stress is a necessary part of living and growing. However, ongoing or severe stress can be very hard on us because of how it affects our mood, our bodies, our relationships, and our resilience—our ability to pick ourselves up and keep going when life gets challenging. Too much stress for too long can put our nervous systems in an overwhelmed state, and we are less able to easily bounce back. It becomes hard to consider our options or to respond in a way that helps us. In this state, we go "offline," meaning that we can't see things or think very clearly. This often happens automatically, without our awareness. Mindful awareness can help us come back "online"— able to see our stress level, signals, and triggers. We can figure out whether a stressor is real or a false alarm, and what we actually need to do to manage our reactions and take care of ourselves.

The first step in this process is to learn how to identify our stress level.

what to try

We can think of stress as occurring over a range from little "s" stress to big "S" stress. Experiencing stress as little or big may depend on how you see it, how long a stressor lasts, its intensity, and whether you are faced with a bunch of stressors at once. For example, little "s" stress might be the reaction to missing a phone call or forgetting to do your laundry. Big "S" stress could be anything from reacting to missing an important test or interview; having a fight with your best friend; being in a pandemic, natural disaster, or some other major crisis that's much bigger than you; or experiencing illness or family problems.

Let's pick a few things that have stressed you out and how intense they felt. Write them in the stress intensity scale below. Try to find at least one stressful event for each level.

A: All right _____

B: Bugged _____

C: Coping _____

D: Dragged down _____

E: Extremely stressed _____

F: Freaked _____

Often, the longer stress lasts, the harder it is on us. Take a moment to look at this list and think about how long the stress lasted (minutes, hours, days, weeks, or ongoing). Write the following letters beside the items you put on the scale: S for short, L for long, and O for ongoing.

more to try

List ten things that stress you out. They could start inside you (pain in your stomach, lack of sleep, a worry). They could start outside you (a car whizzing by you when you are on your bike, or being told you have to give a presentation). They could start from an interaction with another person (an argument, a misunderstanding, a request).

1. _____

2. _____

3. _____

4. _____

5. _____

6. _____

7. _____

8. _____

9. _____

10. _____

Now, next to the stressors you identified, write where it came from: I = inside; O = outside; R = a relationship.

So now you have identified that stress reactions can have different intensities and durations, and that they can come from inside or outside or from your interactions. You may notice that there are some stressors you can change and some you can't. And the number of stressors you are dealing with at the same time can also affect your stress level. All this information can tell you how to best cope with the stress you feel.

11 your coping strategies

what to know

You are probably already using lots of coping skills for managing your stress. Taking a time-out or going for a walk, talking to a friend, or physical exercise can be positive ways to manage a stressed state. If they reduce your stress level, you are better able to move forward with what you have to do.

Some coping strategies are great in the short run but less effective in the long run; for example, procrastination, or putting off doing things that stress you out. Your stress may seem lower at the moment, but it often gets worse the longer you put off the thing you've decided not to do.

It is also common for people to react to stress in a way that can be harmful or problematic, like negative self-talk, binge eating, using alcohol or other drugs, or hitting something.

How do you typically manage the stress you feel? It's good to know what you are doing that is working and what is not. This knowledge can help you decide what might be a good idea to keep doing and what might be better to stop or change.

what to try

Getting to know your coping strategies can help you create a toolkit for managing your stress in healthy ways.

In moments of stress or difficulty, what do you usually do that has been helpful?

_____

_____

_____

_____

_____

List the strategies that are usually helpful, those that are only helpful in the short term, and those that cause you problems. You can download this tool at http://www.newharbinger.com/49432 and print it so that you can keep it handy.

My Coping Strategies for Stress

Helpful	Temporary relief	Problematic

What would you like to change about how you cope with stress?

_____

_____

_____

_____

What do you think gets in the way of responding to stress the way you would like to?

_____

_____

_____

_____

Now that you know your coping strategies and how you might expand them, let's take a look at some of the skills for dealing with stress that you have learned so far.

more to try

We have covered a lot of ways we can use mindfulness exercises and practices to increase our awareness of experience and help us manage stressful moments. Checking in with your thoughts, emotions, and impulses can help you pause, step back, and get a more balanced view of stressors and stress, where you might otherwise have just reacted or lashed out. And bringing mindful attitudes to the moment, like patience or kindness, can shift how you experience stress and how you treat yourself. For example, being intentionally more patient with yourself when you are learning something new can actually reduce the stress you feel and make the learning process easier.

Can you think of any ideas or practices you can use from this workbook? You can go back to sections on mindful attitudes, the STOP practice, the mindful check-in; many people have used these for managing or coping with their stress, and they can be part of your stress toolkit.

Write down which practices you are most likely to use and in what situations:

_____

_____

_____

_____

_____

_____

_____

dealing with little "s" stress 12

what to know

Not all stressors are equal and most of the time we are dealing with little "s" stress, the small things that bug us—like when you can't find your phone, or you're late for a date, or running for the bus. The first step to coping better anytime we are stressed is to slow down, and then to become aware of how stress is showing up and how we are reacting.

Some unhelpful ways of coping include overthinking or worry. It's as if you think you can control or fix a situation by thinking over and over about the bad things that could happen but usually don't. Worrying feels like you are doing something to solve the problem, but it doesn't fix anything and can actually increase your stress.

If a strategy like worrying isn't working, we need to try something different that may be more helpful and get us unstuck. Paying attention to and exploring your body's stress signals (such as tension or shallow breathing) can do three important things. It can shift attention away from unhelpful thinking because we start paying attention to what's happening in the body rather than going down the mind's rabbit hole. It can also give us some important information about how stress is affecting us at the moment. And it gives us an opportunity to pause and *recognize* that we are stressed, *reflect* on what is happening, and take steps to *reset* ourselves to *respond* in a more helpful way of responding. You can think of these as the 4 Rs—**r**ecognize, **r**eflect, **r**eset, **r**espond.

To practice the 4 Rs, it's useful to bring some mindful attitudes to stressful moments. By bringing some acceptance, curiosity, and kindness, instead of trying to escape, resist, or avoid, you can increase your ability to handle the situations you face, and build your resilience.

what to try

Here is a short mindfulness practice that gives you something different to try in those moments you're feeling stress. It's especially helpful for a little "s" stress that is happening in everyday life—something that's a little tough to deal with, like a test, a performance at school, or the thought of asking your crush to hang out with you sometime, but isn't an emergency.

First, catch it (recognize): Pause and notice that you're feeling stressed, recognizing there are signals from your thoughts, emotions, and/or body sensations. The pause interrupts automatic reactions and gives you time to consider your options.

Second, pay attention and investigate (reflect): Ask yourself, "What is here?" Turning attention toward your stress reaction with some curiosity gives you more accurate information about what is going on.

Third, take a moment to center yourself (reset): Take a deeper breath or two to help you slow down and take a step back from your reaction. This can take the charge or heat out of it so you can get some perspective.

Fourth, decide what is needed (respond): You can then purposely, not automatically, choose how to respond and be the boss of your brain. Ask the questions: Can I stop thinking about it and move on? Can I just accept that's the way it is? Do I need to respond? If yes, how do I do that in a way that is best for me?

How might this work in daily life? Casey texted a new friend about getting together to study but didn't hear back for a few hours. Here is how he used this practice to check in and get some space from getting caught up in his reaction.

"Why am I feeling anxious? I need to stop and check in." (Recognize)

"Maybe she doesn't want to study with me? Maybe she doesn't like me. So, that's what I'm thinking. Yeah, I'm feeling so stressed and anxious. Now I need to check in with how my body is feeling. My jaw is tight and so are my shoulders. I feel hot and my stomach kind of hurts." (Reflect)

"I need to take a breath. Okay, that's what is here. Let me just sit with this for a minute." (Reset)

"I'll wait for a while longer, think about it a bit—maybe she's just busy—and then I'll text her again." (Respond)

Using this practice, Casey was able to avoid getting into an automatic reaction that would normally make him feel worse and maybe make the issue bigger. With some patience (sitting with it) and taking a few intentional breaths (calming himself), he was able to think more clearly about how to respond. This gave him a more balanced view.

When you catch some signals that you are reacting to something mildly stressful, try the 4 Rs and notice what happens. Was it helpful? Like any new skill, it tends to work better as you practice it repeatedly.

more to try

So you've checked in and caught yourself in a stress reaction that you've decided isn't helping you. How else might you shift or do a reset to have better perspective or more resources to either let go of overthinking or to handle the situation?

To deal with stress, you need energy and perhaps a different way to approach it. Sometimes you just need a break from it. You've written down some of your coping strategies that seem to work best in a previous activity. Now it's time to consider adding to this list so you have lots to choose from when you need them.

Here's a list of some stress-busting strategies that people often find useful. Check the ones you might try and feel free to write in some of your own on the blank lines.

Switch to being mode; get into your senses.

☐ Mindfully—with your full attention:

take a bath or shower

play your instrument

take a walk in nature

take pictures with your phone

paint or draw or color

☐ Meditate on the breath or do another meditation, using the senses or body sensations, such as the body scan you'll find at http://www.newharbinger .com/49432

☐ Lie in the sun

☐ Play with a pet

☐ Sing loudly to your favorite song

☐ Take a break from social media and step into the world by using your senses

☐ _____

☐ _____

☐ _____

☐ _____

Meet stress with some perspective and kindness to yourself.

☐ Write down your thoughts, emotions, body sensations, and urges. Journaling often takes the heat out of the issues or gives you a little distance from them, which is a great strategy.

☐ Take a more balanced view—write down the reasons why what you are thinking or worrying about might not be true.

☐ Talk to a friend about your worries.

☐ Make a list of things you can do that may be helpful.

☐ Write down the qualities or skills you have that will be useful in the situation.

☐ _____

☐ _____

☐ _____

☐ _____

Work off all that reactive energy.

☐ Run, walk, play a sport.

☐ Work out.

☐ Do yoga.

☐ Dance.

☐ Accomplish some task—clean up, do some laundry, cook something, get something you need at the store.

☐ Cry or yell if you need to.

☐ _____

☐ _____

☐ _____

☐ _____

Over the next week or so, try to use some of the strategies you identified when little-s stress arises. And here, journal a bit about the result. What happened? Did the 4 Rs and the stress-busting strategies you used help you stay mindful and deal with the stress better?

_____

_____

_____

_____

_____

_____

_____

dealing with big "s" stress

what to know

If you have been regularly checking in with your inner world, you'll have noticed that your states—your thoughts, emotions, and body sensations—change all the time. These states are always coming and going as we react to the world and other people. And some states are more comfortable than others.

One way to think of these different states is to put them on a scale like we have before.

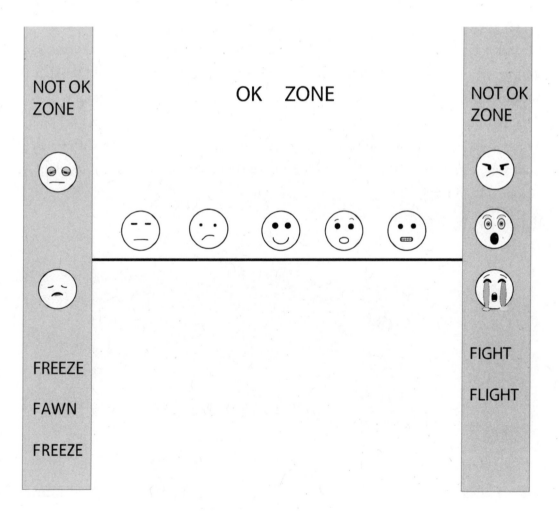

When we are feeling safe and comfortable, let's call that the OK zone. We are able to be open and take in information, and we feel we have the resources to cope with what is happening, whether it's pleasant or unpleasant. However, sometimes we get triggered or feel threatened and we find ourselves outside our OK zone. This may happen when we are dealing with big "S" stress—which could be one really stressful event we're facing, or stress that is really intense, comes from too many sources at once, or lasts for too long. When we're facing big "S" stress, we can get overwhelmed. Often, we're not thinking well anymore. Our body/mind reacts, and our nervous system—the system that regulates our body and the way we react to things—can go into fight-or-flight mode, where we might feel agitated, anxious, or enraged.

On the other side of the scale, we can go into freeze mode, where we might feel numb, unmotivated, and disconnected. We may also go into fawn or flop mode where we avoid conflict, collapse, or give up. These states can be scary. But it's also just part of being human—and this nervous system reaction can also be helpful for our survival when what we're dealing with is really tough, and feeling intense panic and distress would make it that much harder. Still, we don't always need to let it control us. Sometimes the state will just pass; sometimes it's a signal that there really is a problem you have to deal with. And at other times it's an overreaction that you would be better off rethinking or responding to differently if you can. Either way, you want to manage these stress reactions well and get back into the OK zone where you deal with things best.

what to try

This next practice, the mindful shift (inspired by Segal, Williams, and Teasdale 2002, 2013), is for big "S" stress. It can help get you back online when your emotional state is controlling your brain and body.

Here are a series of steps to guide you through an intense stress reaction. (For an audio recording of this practice to get familiar with the steps, visit http://www.newharbinger.com/49432. The recording can be especially useful when you're first starting out with this skill, though you'll eventually want to make this practice one you can do entirely on your own, anytime you notice a difficult state is present.)

NOTE: If at any time this mindfulness practice feels too intense or overwhelming, remember that there are skillful ways to work with this—perhaps opening your eyes if they are closed, looking around the room you are in, naming some objects you see and noticing their colors, shapes, and textures. Or using your sense of touch to ground you in this moment—placing your palms together or on your lap and applying gentle pressure throughout the palm and fingers. Or intentionally pushing your feet into the floor, noting the sensations arising. Or using the breath by deepening your inhale and lengthening your exhale. And if needed you can always stop the practice and take a break. Some other ideas are outlined below in the More to Try section.

Follow these steps in a moment when you are feeling stressed, low, agitated, anxious, or aggravated:

> Briefly notice what is here in thoughts, emotions, and sensations. A few seconds may be enough, and then you can move on to the next step.

> If there are emotions, name them… perhaps saying "Sadness is here," "Anxiety is here," or "Irritation is here," whatever they are… (Remember, name it to claim it! Owning and identifying your emotions can be empowering.)

> Next, bring attention to any body sensations you are aware of, with curiosity. Actually feel your emotions in your body, staying there and exploring them—being with whatever is there the best you can, even if it's unpleasant. Maybe saying to yourself, "This is a moment of stress and difficulty. It's okay, let me feel this. It's okay, this is what's here. I can be with this." If the emotions and body sensations are particularly challenging, note that. If needed, perhaps breathing with them on the in-breath and releasing as best you can on the out-breath, staying with these sensations and emotions for as long as they hold your attention.

> And when you're ready, move your attention from the particular body sensation and bring it to the sensations of breathing at the belly.

> Widen attention to the entire body now, from the top of the head to the tips of the toes, bringing a bigger, open awareness to experience; maybe checking in with what you notice now.

With this practice, you've disrupted what's automatic with a mindful pause, *recognizing* and *reflecting* on what's here by identifying thoughts, naming emotions, and exploring body sensations. *Resetting*, by attending to the sensations of breathing, and then widening attention to the entire body can help us *respond* from an expanded perspective.

Now, think about what you need, or how you could respond in your best interest. Here are some questions you can ask yourself and some possible responses to figure out what to do next.

Let it go?

These thoughts are just thoughts, not facts.

I'm overthinking this.

I don't really need to pay attention to this now because I don't know what's going to happen.

Let it be?

This is hard for me. I may not be able to "fix" this but I can be kind to myself.

That's just the way it is. I know that all things come and go.

Do I need to do something about this?

Do I really understand this?

Do I need to make a plan for responding, maybe when I'm not all caught up in reacting to it?

How do I shift my state or attention so that I don't get stuck in a reaction that's not helpful?

This is too much right now.

I'm just going around in circles. How do I shift, calm, or look after myself?

Building the capacity to stay with discomfort is a superpower that you can develop over time. It is a very different way of dealing with difficulty than many of us typically use, which is to immediately try to fix the problem (which often doesn't work) or get away from it. The mindful shift allows you to stay with your reaction long enough to know what is actually required, and ask, "Can the problem be changed or do I need to change my reaction?" Remember that this is a learned skill that requires some practice to be effective and available to you when you need it.

more to try

Say you do the mindful shift and you realize you've gone way out of your OK zone. Even if you've asked yourself the questions and determined what you might want to try next, you have to recover your sense of emotional balance and bring yourself back online before you can do anything.

There are some strategies that can help you do this. One is to shift to an activity that can help bring you back to your OK zone, like drinking a glass of water, holding some ice cubes, splashing water on your face, taking a few slow breaths, putting on some music you like, doing something physical like walking or dancing, or calling a friend.

There are also some specific grounding exercises that can be helpful in the moment, like focusing on the sensations in your feet as they meet the floor, paying attention to your hands (and touching them if helpful) for a few minutes, or looking at and labeling different objects in the room, using your senses. Grounding practices have a different purpose than the mindfulness practices we have been doing, where we are observing and learning from what is going on without immediately trying to change or fix it. With grounding, our intention or goal is to actually change our state when we need to, in order to get back into our OK zone.

Take a few minutes to get familiar with the well-known grounding exercise on the following page. Then, try it the next time you feel outside your OK zone, to get back to that space of mindful thinking and action. Practicing this over time will make it more effective for you when you need it.

Notice **5 things you can see**. Look around you and become aware of your environment. Be aware of the shape, color, depth, and other visual information.

Notice **4 things you can feel physically**. Bring attention to whatever you're currently feeling, such as the texture of your clothing or the smooth surface of the table you're resting your hands on.

Notice **3 things you can hear**. Listen for sounds. It could be the birds chirping outside or an appliance humming in the next room.

Notice **2 things you can smell**. Bring attention to scents, pleasant or unpleasant. Catch a whiff of any scent in the room or food cooking in the kitchen.

Finally, notice **1 thing you can taste**. Take a sip of a drink, chew gum, or notice the taste in your mouth.

You can create a self-care "kit" (in a pouch or bag) with things in it that engage your senses when you want to focus and ground your attention. This kit is another way to help you shift your state toward the OK zone when you decide that is what you need to do.

What small things can you put in your kit that you can use to fully engage your senses in a positive way? Think of things you have at home or that are easy to get. They could be things like sour candies, a tea you like, chocolate (taste); fuzzy socks, a smooth stone, a squishy ball (touch); and a candle (sight or smell). Just make sure the objects are particular to you, depending on which senses are strongest for you.

Whatever you end up putting in your kit, keep in mind that objects can become less engaging when they are used for a while. If you find an object in your kit isn't working as well as it once did, it may be time to switch it for something else. What's important is to know what is working for you.

In the next chapter, we'll look at ways to help you take care of yourself.

CHAPTER 5

Caring for You

We want to create the conditions that help us be strong and balanced, manage challenges, and respond skillfully as best we can. We also want to respond to ourselves with the same care and compassion that we might offer to a friend—especially when things are tough. Acknowledging your own experience of vulnerability or difficulty, and meeting that with some patience and kindness, means you will be in a better position to learn from whatever difficulty you are going through, rather than spending your energy being hard on yourself. A kinder, more understanding attitude isn't only good for you; it's good for your relationships too. Developing some resilience and patience for ourselves when we are having difficulty actually makes it easier for others to connect with and support us. We can also appreciate that others have similar experiences, and we can give that care and compassion more easily to them.

Although many of us often do not make self-care a priority, the good news is that care for the self and others increases our ability to manage setbacks and our sense of well-being, keeping our battery charged for handling the stress that comes our way.

14 keeping your battery charged

what to know

Nobody handles challenges, difficulties, or stressful situations well when they don't have much in the way of energy or resources. Self-care not only gives us strength and a sense of well-being but also protects us from getting drained when we do have to handle stress. Mindful awareness—checking in with our inner world—is a first step in knowing when we need more self-care to keep our battery charged. Instead of following our habits automatically, awareness allows for the second step: making some intentional choices about how to take care of ourselves and build our resilience for stress.

what to try

Find out what charges your battery or drains it by doing this exercise. You may be surprised at what you find. In the first column, make a list of things you do on an average day, from when you get up in the morning until you go to bed at night; for example, get up, have breakfast, get dressed, and so on. See if you can get around fifteen things on the list.

In the next column, rate each activity as E, D, or 0. Use

E if it gives you *energy* or lightens your mood;

D if it *drains* your energy or drops your mood;

0 if it is *neutral*—doesn't have one effect or the other.

In the Type column, next to the activities that are Es, put A, P, or S. Use

A for *accomplishing* something (it can be a small thing);

P if it gives you *pleasure*;

S if it's *social*.

Activity	Rating	Type

What did you notice or learn from doing this exercise?

_____

_____

_____

Were you surprised by anything being energizing, draining, or neutral? Did you see any patterns?

_____

_____

_____

How is the balance of Es to Ds? Does it need some adjusting to keep you balanced and resilient?

_____

_____

_____

Usually people find that accomplishing something (even if it's really small), doing something that gives them pleasure, or making a positive social connection gives them energy and lifts their mood. If you could plan more of any of these activities in your day, what would they be?

_____

_____

_____

With some choices or planning, you can sometimes do less of the things that drain you or lower your mood. However, some things you can't change—you have to do them. Can you think of a way to make these things less draining—through a change in attitude, making it more interesting or fun by pairing it with something you like, or putting a time limit on it? Come up with a plan that might be doable in the next week as an experiment. Try to make a point of doing one more energizing thing and also change something about one of your draining activities. Write down your plan here.

_____

_____

_____

_____

_____

_____

(Inspired by Segal, Williams, Teasdale 2002, 2013)

more to try

Self-care is not just about what we do. It's also about how we take care of our bodies, mental and emotional health, and our relationships. It's about what inspires us and how we make our lives meaningful. To create a self-care toolkit with a balance of what you need, consider all the areas of your life. This pie chart presents an example.

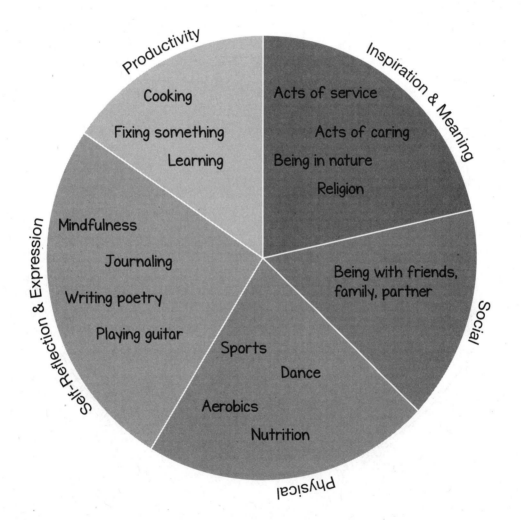

However, everyone's life is unique. Think about what you are doing now that works for you, and also what you may want or need more of to feel at your best. Remember to identify specific activities that you'll use regularly to support you. In this blank pie chart, record the activities (tools) you picked and show how big a piece of your self-care they should be.

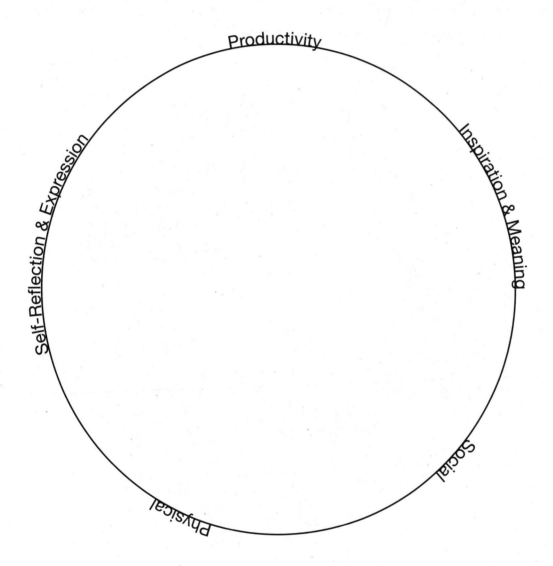

Self-care is a way of being good to yourself and a recognition that you're worth it. Being compassionate toward yourself is another important form of self-care.

what to know

Being compassionate toward yourself is often not so easy. We can be hard on ourselves—do you ever call yourself names or yell at yourself, saying things like "What an idiot!" or "Don't be so stupid!"? Compassion for yourself means knowing when you are suffering and treating yourself kindly, especially when you aren't feeling good. Compassion for yourself means becoming your own friend.

There are a lot of upsides to developing self-compassion. We know, for example, that people who deal with difficult moods are less likely to get stuck in a cycle of negative self-talk that lowers mood and motivation if they are kinder to themselves. They are more likely to bounce back from patterns of reacting to things automatically, and this makes them more resilient (Kuyken 2010). Being resilient means you can recover more quickly from setbacks, such as making a mistake or getting in a fight. That is, you can learn to deal better with what you feel, and get back to doing what you want to do.

Self-compassion starts with mindfulness—you step back and recognize the signals that tell you when you are having difficulty, are stressed, or are judging yourself harshly. Then you bring a kinder, more patient and understanding attitude to yourself. This is how we would want to treat a friend who is struggling and needs some support. You deserve that too.

When you make mistakes, find yourself in difficult situations, or experience distressing emotions, it can also help to acknowledge that you are not alone. This is part of being human, not a failure, or a cause for self-blame or shame. Compassion is what is called for to meet challenges best. If you can practice this, you will be in a much better position to keep some perspective, do what is needed, and move on. The mindful shift in Chapter 3 gives you a formal meditation practice that you can use, or you can just remember to tell yourself (Inspired by Neff, K. 2011):

- I'm in a moment of difficulty.

- Let me be kind and a friend to myself, because that will help me deal with it well.

- Everybody has difficulties. I am not alone.

- What do I need that is really going to help?

what to try

When you find yourself heaping on the self-criticism, blame, or shame, or calling yourself names, try switching it up to something kinder and more encouraging, and still true.

Oh friend...you did it again.

That wasn't my best decision, but...what can I learn from it?

I'm doing the best I can...

This is hard for me....What can I do to help myself?

Or maybe you have a nickname you like, or an endearment someone important to you uses that makes you feel cared about. You can talk to yourself using this more loving name instead of the other harsher ones.

On the lines below, write two kind and encouraging statements you can say to yourself when you are experiencing difficulty and need some self-compassion to face it best. Try them, and then check in with yourself to see how they feel, and if they could be helpful.

_____

_____

_____

_____

Remember the negativity bias you read about in Practice 5? It is actually easier to slip into the destructive habit of calling yourself names. It may, at first, feel weird to say nice things to yourself, but with practice it gets easier and more familiar.

more to try

Touch is known to convey intimacy, love, and compassion (Field 2010). Humans are tactile creatures. While receiving touch from another can be comforting, it may surprise you to know that giving yourself a gentle touch, hug, or squeeze can calm you down and make you feel cared for. You are, in fact, caring for and bringing compassion to yourself.

Try these various kinds of self-touch for ten to thirty seconds each, paying attention to what you notice and what emotions you feel. You can also come up with other ways to soothe yourself through touch. See which ones feel most comfortable for you. You can use these when you are experiencing difficult emotions or just want a different way to take care of yourself. Experiment with them now.

- Stroke your head from your forehead back to the base of your neck.

- Cup your chin and face with both hands and close your eyes.

- Cross your arms and gently stroke up and down your upper arms.

- Give yourself a hug, and kiss one shoulder and then the other.

- Lie down on your back, place one hand in the center of your chest and the other on your belly, and breathe slowly.

- Gently hold your hands in whatever way feels comfortable.

- Give yourself a foot massage.

Was there one or more of these forms of self-touch that you might use? Like everything else, you tend to get a quicker positive response if you practice it. Your nervous system could thank you for this gift to yourself. The suggestion is to try and see if this is helpful.

In the next chapter, we'll look at compassion for others and how to create mindful relationships. Relationships are often our biggest stressors, and they can also be our greatest sources of support. Bringing mindfulness to our interactions with others can enrich our relationships and help us deal with conflict with less stress.

CHAPTER 6

Mindful Communication and Connection

Through mindfulness we can learn some important things about being human. Our minds are very busy judging, analyzing, and comparing ourselves to others. Meanwhile, our physical stress response system is often reacting to a possible threat, even if that threat comes simply from imagining that someone does not like us or approve of us. Having some insight into how we all operate tells us that it's not just us; we are alike and connected. At these times, some compassion for ourselves and others is what is called for. In this chapter, we will bring mindful exploration to how we communicate and connect with each other.

16 HEAR like you're really here; TALK like you really care

what to know

Do you sometimes think people aren't listening to you? Maybe you think that what you've said was misunderstood or ignored. On the other hand, do you ever think that you aren't listening to others? Sometimes, it's not till long after a conversation that you realize you didn't really hear what someone had said to you, or that you made the conversation all about you when you didn't mean to.

You are not alone. There are lots of things that get in the way of actually taking in what people are saying. Other things can be competing for our attention. Often we are planning what we are going to say back, or thinking about something else altogether. It's easy to get lost in our own thoughts when we're trying to listen. Automatically reacting to what is being said is normal (judging, comparing, personalizing, or assuming we know what someone is saying). But it's not how things have to be.

What would mindful listening look like and how would it be helpful in your relationships? Well, what would it be like for you if the person you were talking to were giving you their full attention, without any agenda of their own, and you felt truly heard? Sometimes all we or anyone else needs is a listening ear—and mindful listening can help us learn to provide one.

We can also learn to practice mindful speaking. In conversations, we all say things we wish we could take back. What you say can hurt, anger, or harm someone, even if that wasn't what you meant to do. So it can be helpful to be mindful when speaking—paying attention, really choosing what you are about to say (intention), having a kind attitude.

In this activity, you'll learn two ways to bring mindful attention and attitudes—such as curiosity, patience, nonjudgment, and kindness—to your communication with others so you can have better relationships.

what to try

This HEAR practice is closely aligned with the version described by mindfulness coach Elaine Smookler (2017). The letters in the practice give you a way to remember how to listen mindfully.

Here—Really be *here* and offer your full attention.

Enjoy—*Enjoy* a breath and listen to what is being said, whether you like it or not.

Ask—*Ask* yourself if you really know what the other person means, and ask for clarification if you need it. Bring openness and curiosity to the interaction. You might be surprised at what you discover.

Reflect—*Reflect* back what you heard. This tells the person speaking that you were really listening.

Try it out with a friend or family member in a short conversation. You may notice it's not so easy to fully pay attention, to be open and curious to what someone is saying, but do your best and notice what comes up. Write any observations here:

_____

_____

_____

_____

_____

_____

more to try

The letters in TALK can give you a prompt to speak mindfully when you want to take care with what you're saying.

Take—*Take* a breath and consider your state, what you want to say, and how to say it.

Attitude—Ask yourself, What *attitude* am I bringing to this conversation? Is it helpful or harmful?

Listen—*Listen* to your thoughts about what you want to say. Is it true? Needed? Kind?

Kind—Speak *kindly* to yourself and others as best you can, whether that means sticking up for yourself, acknowledging a problem, or making a point. This is often not easy, but it makes it more likely you will be heard.

Try it out with a friend or family member in a short conversation, particularly if you want to be careful and thoughtful about what you are saying. Write any observations here:

_____

_____

_____

_____

_____

Using HEAR and TALK in your conversations takes practice because it's not our usual, automatic way of communicating. Do your best and notice what comes up. See if it seems easier to really hear other people and be heard yourself.

stressful talks and texts 17

what to know

Mindfulness skills, such as awareness of your own reactions and choosing how to respond instead of reacting, can be really useful when talking or texting with others gets stressful. When we think that something said to us is threatening, aggressive, hurtful, disrespectful, or confusing, we react, even if the person didn't mean it that way. We can get emotionally hijacked. As with any kind of stress, getting caught up in reacting often makes the situation and interaction worse; our thinking, empathy, and judgment goes offline. This is when it's good to have some tools for cooling down, stepping back to get some perspective, and deciding how you want to handle the interaction. One way to do this is to take a mindful pause or a breath and check in with yourself. This pause can also be useful when you're using social media and get triggered by something you experience as challenging or threatening.

what to try

Think of a time when you had a difficult conversation that was distressing. If you were able to slow down and get some perspective, how might it have been different?

Write down the situation. Who was it with? Where were you? When did it happen? Were you texting or face-to-face or on the phone?

_____

_____

_____

What thoughts popped into your head?

_____

_____

_____

What emotions did you have?

_____

_____

What came up in your body?

_____

_____

What do you think was going on for the other person? List as many possibilities as you can, including those that may have had nothing to do with you.

_____

_____

_____

_____

_____

How long did you think about the conversation afterward? What were the upsides and downsides of that?

_____

_____

Can you think of any mindful ways you could have responded?

_____

_____

_____

As you wrote all this down, did you learn anything or see anything differently than you originally did?

18 connection: you and me

what to know

Our differences are important. Our unique background, history, and qualities help make us who we are. Truly connecting with others involves understanding and respecting those differences. At the same time, it's important to see how we, as humans, are more similar than different and are necessarily interconnected. Recognizing this can help us not take things so personally (*This is all about me!*) and be more empathic and compassionate toward others (*There is someone here other than me.*). This recognition can also help us remember to treat ourselves the way we treat others—the way we want to be treated. When we see how interconnected we are, we also realize that we are not alone, even if we sometimes feel that way. And lastly, studies seem to show that the more compassionate we are to ourselves and others, the happier we are.

what to try

The following practice focuses on connection; try it and see what you notice. It's not necessary to feel anything in particular. Simply approach it as an experiment.

Get into a comfortable position, close your eyes for five minutes, and bring attention to your body sitting and any sensations you notice inside the body and at the surface of the skin. Check in with what is present for you now in your thoughts or emotions, and then take a couple of minutes to pay attention to the sensations of your breathing wherever you are most aware of them. Then think of someone you know, perhaps not really well, someone you feel good to neutral about. If you have a picture of them or the two of you, you could have it with you during this practice. Now either seeing this person in your mind or looking at the picture, slowly read *only* the statements in the first column:

They're like me	I'm like them
This person is a human like me.	I'm a human like them.
They have a body, thoughts, and emotions like me.	I have a body, thoughts, and emotions like them.
They pass gas like me.	I pass gas like them.
They laugh like me.	I laugh like them.
They get sad like me.	I get sad like them.
They get mad like me.	I get mad like them.
They get high like me.	I get high like them.
They get low like me.	I get low like them.
They have fears like me.	I have fears like them.
They have tears like me.	I have tears like them.
They want love like me.	I want love like them.
They want joys like me.	I want joys like them.
They have hopes like me.	I have hopes like them.
They eat junk food like me.	I eat junk food like them.
They drink water like me.	I drink water like them.
They need sleep like me.	I need sleep like them.
They have pain like me.	I have pain like them.
They pee and poop like me.	I pee and poop like them.
They wear clothes like me.	I wear clothes like them.
They have things they love like me.	I have things I love like them.
They have things they don't love like me.	I have things I don't love like them.
They need care and kindness like me.	I need care and kindness like them.

Now close your eyes and take a few deep breaths. Opening your eyes again and either holding that person in mind or looking at the picture, slowly read the statements in the column on the right.

Finally, imagine you and the other person together or look at the picture of you together, with thoughts or wishes for the well-being of both of you. Here are some examples:

May we both be happy and loved.

May we both be cared for and care for others.

May we both feel safe and okay.

May we both be kind to ourselves when we're having a hard time.

You can write down other thoughts or wishes that are meaningful to you.

_____

_____

_____

_____

_____

_____

Now close your eyes again, bring the two of you to mind, and slowly repeat the phrase or phrases to yourself several times, pausing in between. Notice what emotions or body sensations come up, if any, as you extend these warm wishes. Then open your eyes, and let go of this practice, moving your body however you want.

Now write down any thoughts or observations you have on this practice.

_____

_____

_____

_____

_____

growing your mindful heart 19

what to know

Can you remember a time when you felt close to a person or a pet and had warm feelings toward them—someone you appreciated, really "saw," and would wish the best for? We all have had this experience, and it makes us feel good. Perhaps you felt your heart open to another being. This warmth goes beyond yourself to the other being and, if you thought about it, you might wish that they were happy, healthy, free from stress and suffering.

There are mindfulness meditations that help us grow these feelings and attitudes so we can have this experience more easily and more often. In this practice, we are intentionally bringing attitudes of kindness and generosity to others. There is no guarantee that you will feel anything. However, with some experimentation and repetition, this state can become more available to you and more automatic, rather than just happening by chance. With practice, you'll develop the habit of connecting with others in this warm and openhearted way.

what to try

You can do this practice with people you know or don't know, or with a pet or any living being, for that matter. The point is to set an intention to bring up caring feelings and warm wishes in yourself toward others. It's not necessary to actually feel anything. As an experiment, try one or more of the following for a week.

Sit and close your eyes for five minutes, having the other person or being you're focusing on in mind, and saying to yourself several times with pauses, as sincerely as possible, "I hope you are okay." See if you can tap into that feeling you have for people you care about, in your heart and body. You can place a hand over your chest if you want to.

As you pass strangers on the street over the next week, try to hold the people you see in mind for a moment, and silently say to yourself, "I hope you are okay." You might do this for five minutes or so once a day, perhaps with five people, when you're on your way somewhere.

At random moments when you are with family or friends, take a moment and say to yourself, "I hope you are okay." Next time you are with such a group, practice this five times during the get-together.

If you have a connection with animals and nature, you can direct your good wishes to them. Pick a specific time, once during the week for five minutes. All beings and living things are deserving of our care and hopes for their well-being, and it's great to turn attention to that. Doing this also contributes to our own happiness.

Whatever you try, notice what comes up for you when you do this and write your observations here:

_____

_____

_____

_____

_____

_____

_____

CHAPTER 7

Moving On

Congratulations for making it to the last part of this mindfulness workbook! Thank you for your efforts and thank yourself for your efforts. This chapter will help you reflect on what you have learned—the mindful awareness, skills, practices, and attitudes—and how you will use this learning in the future.

20 looking back

what to know

Learning works best when we think about what we've learned after we've learned it, and when we remember to apply it in our lives. Whether you did all or some of the practices, it's good to reflect on what you have learned so it is carried forward and useful to you in the future.

what to try

First, think about your experience with this book in general.

Were there any surprises?

_____

_____

_____

What did you notice or learn that you would like to remember going forward?

_____

_____

_____

_____

Do you have any new skills as a result of the different activities and practices you've done?

_____

_____

_____

_____

Here's a list of things we covered to refresh your memory. Put a check next to the information or activities you found most interesting or helpful.

Formal Practices

☐ STOP

☐ Awareness of breath

☐ Mindful check-in

☐ 4 Rs (recognize, reflect, reset, respond)

☐ Mindful shift

☐ Grounding practices (sensing your hands or the soles of your feet, attending to the five senses, or using a self-care kit, when out of the OK zone)

☐ HEAR for mindful listening; TALK for mindful speaking

☐ They're like me; I'm like them

☐ "I hope you're okay" (sitting)

Informal Practices and Skills

☐ Getting curious about and observing your inner world

☐ Identifying thoughts, emotions, and body sensations as they happen

☐ Using opportunities in daily life, like paying attention to your senses while washing dishes, to be mindful

☐ Giving your full attention to a positive experience

☐ Noticing when you are stressed and investigating what is going on in the moment

☐ Exploring mindful attitudes—not judging ourselves so harshly, developing patience and kindness

☐ Using supportive touch for self-compassion

☐ Recognizing when your battery may need charging

☐ "I hope you're okay" (walking, with friends, with family, in nature)

Awareness and Knowledge

☐ Doing and being mode—we can choose

☐ Negativity bias is our default—being aware of that and having some perspective

☐ Learning about emotions—name it to claim it

☐ Understanding how stress works and how you feel it

☐ Knowing your coping strategies for stress and looking at options

☐ Recognizing when you are in an OK zone or out, or in between

☐ Investigating stressful talks and texts

☐ Activities that are energizing or draining—choices

☐ Knowing how to create a self-care plan

☐ Benefits of self-compassion and self-care

Briefly write about a time when you used one of these skills in your day-to-day life after learning about it in this book. What happened? What did the skill allow you to do that you might not have been able to do before?

_____

_____

_____

Was there anything you found that was not so helpful?

_____

_____

_____

more to try

Now it's time to reflect on where you started, what you want to take away, and what that might look like. Let's do this in a particular way. Below is a box where you can draw an outline of your hand. Reflect on your answers to these questions and express them through words, images, or color.

Bottom of the paper: Why did you start this workbook?

Palm: What were your intentions at the beginning? What did you hope to get?

Little finger: What were the most interesting and useful skills, practice, and knowledge?

Ring finger: Has there been any impact on you personally? Do you see anything or react to anything differently?

Middle finger: Has there been any change in your attitude or behavior toward yourself or in your relationships?

Pointer finger: What might help you move forward with a mindfulness practice? (For example, apps, some small daily practice, friends, a mindfulness group)

Thumb: What might get in the way of maintaining some mindfulness practice and using the skills you have learned?

Space above the hand: What are your hopes for your future? How can mindfulness practice support these hopes?

21 looking ahead—your mindfulness practice

what to know

Now you've thought about what you have learned and experienced some of the benefits of bringing mindfulness forward into your life. As you may have noticed, there are many paths to being mindful. Whether you choose to work with an attitude, like curiosity or compassion, or to bring attention and choice to your present-moment experience and reactions, or to use the awareness tools you learned in your relationships, you are practicing mindfulness.

We have identified five areas where you might find opportunities to practice even more mindfulness skills going forward. You can think of these areas as branches on a tree, separate but all related. And as a tree grows from a seed, so, too, can your practice start small and grow strong.

what to try

Opportunities to practice, or OTPs, are moments in our life where we may choose to put mindfulness into action and discover what it might offer (Freedman 2018). We can plan for these opportunities or catch them whenever they come up. Remember, the more OTPs we can bring mindful skills to, the more we are intentionally changing our brains to respond to stress in more helpful or adaptive ways, and the more resilient, calm, and compassionate we will become. To start, read through the descriptions of each branch, then choose one branch that interests you and feels manageable, and pick out one way you'll practice going forward. Planning your practice this way makes it more likely that you'll do it.

- **Responding mindfully**

We can pause to get curious about a pleasant or unpleasant event in the moment, paying attention on purpose, and responding, not reacting automatically. Paying attention to your inner world in this way creates some space between what you're faced with and what you usually or immediately do. This can provide other perspectives about what is going on and more options. You can use the STOP, mindful check-in, or mindful shift practices as tools to create this space.

- **Formal practice**

Most people benefit from structure when learning anything. Formal practices involve a planned time to engage in mindfulness, in a dedicated fashion—perhaps sitting still and using the sensations of breathing as a focus for attention for a period of about fifteen minutes, or a period of mindful movement. There are many kinds of formal practice, or meditation. Formal practices still provide a way to see how we operate as humans and be aware of our individual habits of mind/body/emotions. For example, you can practice watching a thought come up, acknowledging that, and then choosing where you want your attention to be—following the thought, or coming back to your body and what you feel now, or going somewhere else. This helps you train your attention, develop your awareness, and understand yourself better. And ultimately, it helps you to be the boss of your brain. (You can download recordings of some formal practices at http://www.newharbinger.com/49432.)

- **Informal practice**

As we go through our day, we have many opportunities to pay attention on purpose to the present moment and come to our senses, giving our doing mind a break. In other words, informal practice is bringing mindfulness into something we are doing already. For example, when you are eating a piece of chocolate, you might pay full attention to the taste for the first few bites, or the texture of it. Sometimes we just want to shake things up—disrupting our tendency to live in our heads, in the past and future—and informal experiences of mindfulness and close attention to what we're doing and feeling can help us manage this. The other benefit of informal practice is the ability to fully appreciate some of the joys and pleasures of life we might usually miss.

- **Relating mindfully**

There are many opportunities to be mindful of the way you are relating to yourself, others, and the world and to notice how others are relating to you. Notice how you are relating to yourself when you make a mistake. Are you beating yourself up or recognizing that this is an opportunity to learn and grow? Relating mindfully might take the form of interacting with more awareness. You could practice bringing your full attention to what is actually going on in a conversation, without the assumptions and limitations that usually color how we relate, or you could notice how you are relating to the weather. It's raining and you can notice how you are reacting to that, but also pause and consider if you can relate to it differently. With mindfulness or a mindful attitude shift, you might actually choose to respond another way. Singing in the rain?

- **Attitudes**

We can acknowledge that the attitudes we bring to our experiences shape those experiences in both positive and negative ways. They have a big effect on how we see, think, and feel about things. When you encounter things that make you feel angry or sad or tired, it may often seem that what you feel is just what you feel, and there's nothing you can do about it. But guess what? We are actually free to experiment with trying on other attitudes to the things we experience—all of which we can already access.

Say you recognize that you are feeling impatient. Here's your opportunity to pause and try on patience, and see what changes, if anything. And if the answer is "Nothing," and you still feel impatient, that's okay! You may find that the experience of trying on patience makes the impatience a little easier to deal with. Or maybe you've discovered that the thing that makes you impatient is something that really matters to you, and that's *why* you feel impatient. Working with attitudes can give you more information and choices around how you relate to yourself, others, and the world.

What do you think would happen if you worked with one of the mindful attitudes in different situations for a week? When an issue comes up, could you try **getting curious** first instead of reacting, **accepting** the way things are as a starting point instead of wishing they were different, **catching yourself** when you're judging yourself or others harshly, and **letting it go** at least for now (since often, judging yourself and others does more harm than good)?

Which of these five branches do you feel like you might want to experiment with over the next week or so?

_____

What OTPs can you see in this area in your day-to-day life? How will you take advantage of these opportunities over the next week or so?

_____

_____

_____

_____

Once you've had a chance to practice a skill in this area a few times, write about how the experience went. What changed, if anything? How can you continue bringing this skill into your life? Or, if you prefer, you can write about which area of mindfulness you'll want to work on next, and how.

_____

_____

_____

_____

_____

_____

_____

more to try

Making mindfulness a part of your life involves using resources to support your practice. Resources may be internal, such as formal and informal practices, attitudes, and certain personality traits like perseverance, openness, and organization. Others are external, such as people, places, and things.

Focusing on some resources outside yourself, think about the following and put a check next to those that might help you continue living mindfully. Choose one and research it.

People—Are there people in your life who could act as mindfulness buddies? Could you practice and experiment with them using the mindfulness skills you've learned?

Groups—Google mindfulness groups in general or in your area (if you want to meet in person) and see what comes up. Consider doing a mindfulness-based stress reduction group, or if you tend to get anxious or depressed, doing a mindfulness-based cognitive therapy group. If you tend to be really hard on yourself, why not try a mindful self-compassion group?

Apps, podcasts, YouTube, and audio recordings—There are many ways to continue exploring ideas or activities in this workbook that you found interesting and/or helpful. You can search for meditations you might like to listen to; Insight Timer has a lot to choose from and there are many others. We have also provided some short recorded formal practices at http://www.newharbinger.com/49432.

Books—Think about particular aspects of mindfulness you might like to learn more about and check out what's available online or at your local library or bookstore.

more to try

A mindful living contract can be a way to keep your practice alive, motivating you to keep learning how to use the concepts, attitudes, meditations, exercises, and OTPs we have covered.

At http://www.newharbinger.com/49432, you'll find a contract you can download and print.

Write down three intentions you will have to help you live mindfully. Make these intentions manageable and concrete, and make sure they have a defined beginning and end. For example, you might say, "My intention is to do one short awareness of breath practice when I wake up twice this week," or "I intend to engage in mindful listening for five minutes when in conversation today."

My Mindful Living Contract

My intention is to _____

_____

_____ times per week for the next _____ weeks.

My intention is to_____

_____

_____ times per week for the next _____ weeks.

My intention is to_____

_____

_____ times per week for the next _____ weeks.

Once you've written your contract, put it somewhere that you can see it daily to help you make these practices a way of being. You can always change the contract as needed. Consistency of practice for a period of time is helpful for skill building and changing things up also keeps things fresh.

Remember that mindfulness is both a way of doing and a way of being. And remember that a little bit of regular practice is better than no practice at all. The point here is to continue to develop your awareness and skills to see and work with your inner world. Then you have more choice about how to respond, no matter what the situation is—but especially when things are challenging.

Having more ways to deal with difficult emotions and life situations means we may be more able to deal with what we're facing in ways that are healthy and kind and to choose what's best for us. And don't forget that mindfulness also brings us more joy for the little and big things in life; when you are mindful, you are more open and receptive to taking in the awesome.

Mindfulness benefits not only you but also the people around you. Developing the kind of clarity and ability to pay attention that mindfulness gives you allows you to treat yourself and everyone else with more kindness and compassion. We simply need to remember to bring the practice of mindfulness to ourselves, others, and the world.

references

Field, T. 2010. "Touch for Socioemotional and Physical Well-Being: A Review." *Developmental Review* 30: 367–383.

Freedman, M. L. 2018. In conversation, Toronto, Ontario.

Hanson, R. 2009. *Buddha's Brain: The Practical Neuroscience of Happiness, Love and Wisdom.* Oakland, CA: New Harbinger Publications.

Kabat-Zinn, J. 1990. *Full Catastrophe Living: Using the Wisdom of Your Body and Mind to Face Stress, Pain, and Illness.* New York: Delacorte Press.

Kuyken, W., E. Watkins, E. Holden, K. White, R. S. Taylor, S. Byford, A. Evans, S. Radford, J. D. Teasdale, and T. Dalgleish. 2010. "How Does Mindfulness-Based Cognitive Therapy Work?" *Behaviour Research and Therapy* 48(11):1105–12.

Neff, K. 2011. *Self-Compassion: The Proven Power of Being Kind to Yourself.* Harper Collins.

Segal, Z. V., J. M. Williams, and J. D. Teasdale. 2002. *Mindfulness-Based Cognitive Therapy for Depression: A New Approach to Preventing Relapse.* New York: Guilford Press.

———. 2013. *Mindfulness-Based Cognitive Therapy for Depression.* 2nd ed. New York: Guilford Press.

Selye, H. 1973. "The Evolution of the Stress Concept: The Originator of the Concept Traces Its Development from the Discovery in 1936 of the Alarm Reaction to Modern Therapeutic Applications of Syntoxic and Catatoxic Hormones." *American Scientist,* 61(6), 692–699.

Smookler, E. 2017. "How to Practice Mindful Listening." *Mindful Magazine,* February issue number 24, Anthem Publishing. Online March 2017, Retrieved from mindful.org/how-to-practice-mindful-listening/August 25, 2021.

Woods, S. L., P. Rockman, and E. Collins. 2019. *Mindfulness-Based Cognitive Therapy: Embodied Presence and Inquiry in Practice.* Oakland, CA: New Harbinger Publications.

acknowledgments

We would like to express our gratitude to the great lineage and community of mindfulness teachers, our teachers in particular (you know who you are), and the Centre for Mindfulness Studies. Without them this workbook would not be possible. We would also like to recognize all of the front-line workers and youth that participated in and helped shape the Grow Mindfulness for Youth Project, developed from a grant from the Ontario Trillium Foundation (OTF) and produced by the Centre for Mindfulness Studies Community Program. They also inspired this workbook. Finally, we would like to acknowledge those young people who gave us input through their stories and feedback on the manuscript. These people include Taylor Young, Casey Fulford, Jennifer MacDermid, and Heather Sorenson.

Patricia Rockman, MD, is a family physician with a focused practice in mental health. She is associate professor in the department of family and community medicine at the University of Toronto, and cofounder of the Centre for Mindfulness Studies in Toronto, ON, Canada. She is a public speaker, curriculum developer, and teaches and mentors in mindfulness-based cognitive therapy (MBCT) and mindfulness-based stress reduction (MBSR).

Allison McLay, DCS, RP, is a registered psychotherapist, and faculty at the Centre for Mindfulness Studies. She teaches MBSR and MBCT, and trains health care providers to deliver these modalities. She was an author in curriculum development for the youth mindfulness program at the Centre for Mindfulness Studies.

M. Lee Freedman, MD, CM, FRCP(C), is a Toronto-based child, adolescent, and family psychiatrist. She is experienced in integrating mindfulness training into her therapeutic work with youth and adults in need of help with mental health challenges.